INDIANA UNIVERSITY

JOSH ANDERSON

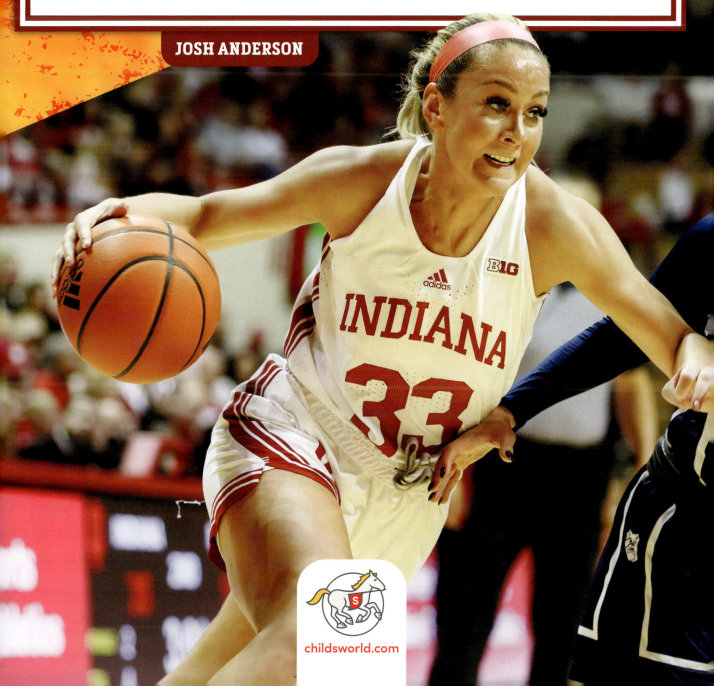

childsworld.com

Published by The Child's World®
800-599-READ • www.childsworld.com

Copyright © 2024 by The Child's World®
All rights reserved. No part of this book may be reproduced or utilized in any form or by any means without written permission from the publisher.

Photography Credits
page 1: ©SOPA Images/Contributor/Getty Images; page 2: ©Ethan Miller/Staff/Getty Images; page 5: ©YHoshua/Wikimedia; page 7: ©NCAA Photos/Contributor/Getty Images; page 8: ©Marcus Mote/Indiana State Library, Indiana Division; page 9: ©Icon Sports Wire/Contributor/Getty Images; page 11: ©Andy Lyons/Staff/Getty Images; page 12: ©Icon Sportswire/Contributor/Getty Images; page 15: ©Rich Clarkson/Contributor/Getty Images; page 16: ©Bettmann/Contributor/Getty Images; page 17: ©JOHN RUTHROFF/Contributor/Getty Images; page 18: ©Icon Sportswire/Contributor/Getty Images; page 19: ©Carmen Mandato/Staff/Getty Images; page 21: ©Icon Sportswire/Contributor/Getty Images; page 23: ©Jonathan Daniel/Stringer/Getty Images; page 24: ©NCAA Photos/Contributor/Getty Images; page 27: ©Andy Lyons/Staff/Getty Images; page 28: ©Justin Casterline/Stringer/Getty Images; page 29: ©Mark Blinch/Contributor/Getty Images

ISBN Information
9781503885219 (Reinforced Library Binding)
9781503885455 (Portable Document Format)
9781503886094 (Online Multi-user eBook)
9781503886735 (Electronic Publication)

LCCN 2023937754

Printed in the United States of America

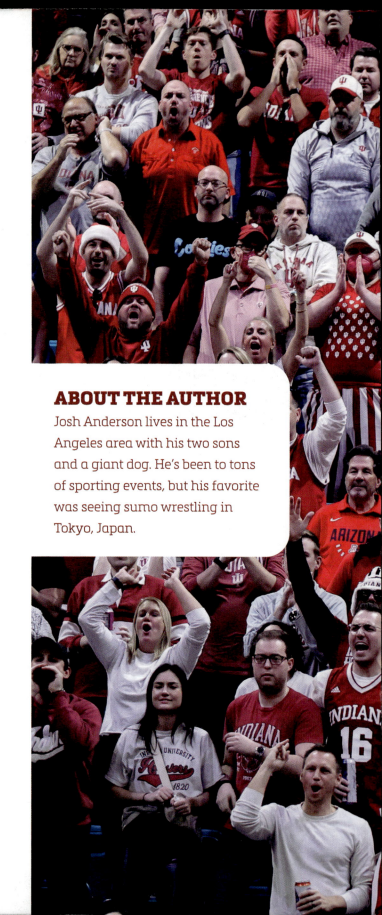

ABOUT THE AUTHOR

Josh Anderson lives in the Los Angeles area with his two sons and a giant dog. He's been to tons of sporting events, but his favorite was seeing sumo wrestling in Tokyo, Japan.

CONTENTS

CHAPTER ONE
Origins . . . 4

CHAPTER TWO
Rivalries . . . 10

CHAPTER THREE
Great Moments . . . 14

CHAPTER FOUR
All-Time Greats . . . 20

CHAPTER FIVE
The Modern Era . . . 26

Glossary . . . 30

Fun Facts . . . 31

One Stride Further . . . 31

Find Out More . . . 32

Index . . . 32

CHAPTER ONE

Origins

Indiana University (IU) opened its doors in Bloomington, Indiana, in 1825. The school was first called State Seminary. The name changed to Indiana College in 1828. Then, it became Indiana University in 1838. Indiana became one of the first state universities in the United States to admit women in 1867. In 1883, the school's original **campus** burned down. Its new campus was rebuilt nearby. The school remains in that location today. The university is home to more than 45,000 students.

All teams at Indiana are called Hoosiers. While the school does not have a mascot, the men's and women's basketball teams have a very interesting tradition beloved by fans of the team. The players wear red-and-white striped pants before each game.

The first Hoosiers men's basketball team won only one of their five games in 1900–01.

Men's basketball started at Indiana during the 1900–01 season. Indiana basketball has been part of the **NCAA**'s Big Ten **Conference** since the team began. Indiana won its first national championship in 1940 under coach Branch McCracken. They won another in 1953. The school's other three national championships came under Coach Bobby Knight between 1976 and 1987. Indiana's five titles are tied with Duke University for the fourth-most of all time. Indiana is often one of the best teams in the Big Ten.

Indiana University Hoosiers

TEAM NAME: Indiana Hoosiers

FIRST SEASON: 1900 (Men's Team); 1971 (Women's Team)

CONFERENCE: Big Ten

CONFERENCE CHAMPIONSHIPS: 22 (Men's Team); 2 (Women's Team)

HOME ARENA: Simon Skjodt Assembly Hall

NCAA TOURNAMENT APPEARANCES: 41 (Men's Team); 9 (Women's Team)

NATIONAL CHAMPIONSHIPS: 5 (Men's Team); 0 (Women's Team)

The Indiana and Kansas men's teams do battle in the 1953 National Championship. Indiana won 69-68.

ORIGIN OF TEAM NAME

Since the school was founded, teams at Indiana have been called the Hoosiers. There are several theories about how the name started. One involves a man named Mr. Hoosier, who was working on a canal located in Louisville, Kentucky. Mr. Hoosier preferred to hire workers from Indiana. These workers came to be called "Hoosier's men." The term stuck and is still used today as a word for people from Indiana.

But the men's team hasn't made it past the **Sweet 16** round of the **NCAA Tournament** since 2002. That year, Indiana lost to the University of Maryland in the national championship game.

Women started playing basketball at the school as far back as the early 1900s. But the school did not have an official women's basketball team until 1971. The women's Hoosiers team joined the Big Ten Conference in 1982. They competed in the NCAA Tournament for the first time in 1983. Today, the women's team is often at the top of the Big Ten. The 2022–23 team finished with a 28–4 record, the best in school history. While the team hasn't yet been to the **Final Four** or won a national title, the women's Hoosiers team is on the right track.

Indiana guard Alexis Gassion (right) passes the ball in a game against Ohio State.

CHAPTER TWO

Rivalries

Indiana's main basketball rival is the Purdue Boilermakers. Rivals are teams that have a long history of playing each other for the right to claim they are the best. Purdue is about 100 miles (161 kilometers) from Indiana's campus. The men's and women's teams play each other at least twice each season. Since the Hoosiers and Boilermakers both play in the Big Ten, they sometimes play a third time in the conference tournament.

The first game between the men's basketball teams from the two schools was in 1901. Purdue won 20–15. Of the 217 games between the men's teams, Purdue has won 125, while Indiana has won 92. Although Purdue has won more games in the rivalry's history, Indiana has won the national title five times. Purdue has never been the national champion.

The Hoosiers hosted Purdue in the teams' first meeting of the 2021–22 season. Indiana was hoping to earn their first trip to the NCAA Tournament since 2016. Purdue was **ranked** number four in the entire country.

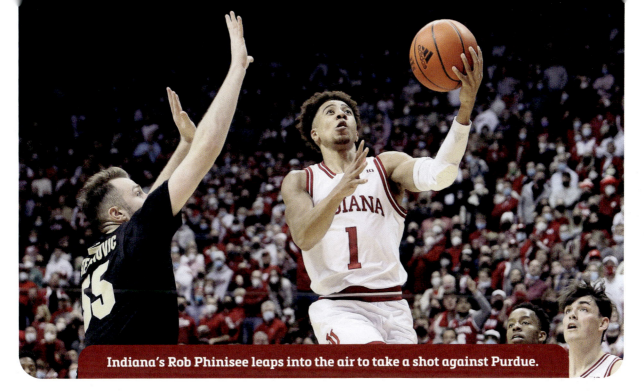
Indiana's Rob Phinisee leaps into the air to take a shot against Purdue.

Purdue had won the last nine meetings between the teams. Even though the game was at Indiana, the Boilermakers were favored to win.

After Indiana took an 11-point lead in the first half, Purdue came back in the second. A jump shot by Purdue guard Jaden Ivey tied the game 63–63 with just over three minutes to go. Neither team scored for more than two minutes before Purdue took a 65–63 lead on a layup by forward Mason Gillis. Then, Indiana guard Rob Phinisee hit a three-pointer with 18 seconds left to put the Hoosiers up 66–65. Two free throws made the Hoosiers' lead 68–65. As time ran out, Purdue missed a three-point shot that would have won the game. The Indiana crowd stormed the court to celebrate the end of Indiana's losing streak to Purdue.

Since 2001–02, Indiana's women have won 19 of their 44 games against Purdue.

Indiana's women's team has played Purdue 93 times. Purdue has won 53 of those games. The two teams met for the first time in 1972. While Indiana won 18 of their first 20 meetings with the Boilermakers, Purdue has had a serious advantage ever since.

The first meeting of the 2021–22 season between the women's Hoosiers and Boilermakers teams was a classic matchup in the rivalry between the teams. The game took place on Purdue's home court. The Hoosiers were ranked sixth in the country and were expected to win. But anything is possible in a game between heated rivals.

Purdue led 32–27 at the half before Indiana tied the game at the end of the third quarter. Then, in the fourth, Purdue's Abbey Ellis hit a three-pointer with just over three minutes left in the game. The shot put the Boilermakers up 55–47. But Indiana roared back. A three-pointer by Ali Patberg with 19 seconds left brought the score to 59–58. Indiana was one point from a win, but foul shots tied the game 60–60. The game went to overtime. Two Indiana three-pointers helped seal the 73–68 win for the Hoosiers.

While Kentucky, Illinois, and Michigan State also count among Indiana's rivals, there is no foe the Hoosier fans love to beat more than the Purdue Boilermakers.

First Meeting:
1901 (Men's Teams); 1972 (Women's Teams)

Indiana's Record against Purdue:
92–125 (Men's); 41–55 (Women's)

CHAPTER THREE

Great Moments

The 1975-76 Hoosiers men's team is considered to be one of the greatest to ever play college basketball. The team featured six future National Basketball Association (NBA) players. They were ranked first in the country all season. The Hoosiers finished the season with a perfect 32-0 record.

Indiana's 1986-87 men's team is also one of the best in school history. They finished the regular season with a 24-4 record and fought their way through the NCAA Tournament. The Hoosiers made it to the final game and were up against the Syracuse Orangemen. The winner would be that year's national champion.

The game was close. With 38 seconds left, Syracuse took a 73-70 lead. Indiana guard Keith Smart grabbed a rebound, dribbled the length of the court, and scored. After Syracuse failed to score, Indiana got the ball back with a chance to win the game. Leading scorer Steve Alford couldn't find a shot. Smart got the ball and dribbled into the left corner.

Legendary Indiana coach Bobby Knight instructs Kent Benson during a 1975 game. Benson went on to play 11 seasons in the NBA, and Knight was head coach of the Hoosiers for almost 30 years.

With four seconds left, Smart launched a game-winning shot that swished through the net. Indiana won the national championship 74–73. Smart's final shot is one of the greatest plays in the history of college basketball.

One of the biggest moments in the history of the Hoosiers women's team came during the 2021 NCAA Tournament. The women's Hoosiers made the Sweet 16 round for only the second time in school history. Coach Teri Moren hoped to lead the team to the **Elite Eight** for the first time. Indiana was matched up with the top team in their region, the North Carolina (NC) State Wolfpack.

The Hoosiers built a 10-point lead in the third quarter, with top scorer Ali Patberg leading the charge. Although Indiana still led by 10 with just under 3 minutes left to play, NC State scored the next 8 points, bringing the score to 70–68.

◀ Indiana's Keith Smart sinks the game-winning basket of the 1987 NCAA Championship game.

THAT'S STRANGE!

There's a definite connection between Indiana college basketball and the city's NBA team, the Pacers. Bobby "Slick" Leonard was the captain of Indiana's 1953 championship team. Isiah Thomas led the Hoosiers to the title in 1981. Calbert Cheaney is the all-time leading scorer in Indiana men's basketball history. Amazingly, all three went on to coach the Indiana Pacers. Leonard coached the team from 1968 to 1980. Thomas coached from 2000 to 2003. And Cheaney was hired as an assistant coach in 2020. Even Larry Bird, who played for Indiana State, not Indiana University, coached the Pacers for three seasons!

17

Hoosier Ali Patberg lines up a free throw.

The Hoosiers women's team celebrates their Sweet 16 victory over the North Carolina State Wolfpack in 2021.

After Indiana hit a pair of free throws, Wolfpack guard Raina Perez hit a jumper. Patberg was fouled on the next play and hit one of two free throws, putting the Hoosiers up 73–70. NC State star center Elissa Cunane took a three-pointer with time running out that would've tied the game. But she missed the shot, and Indiana advanced to the Elite Eight for the first time in team history. Even though they lost to Arizona in their next game, the Elite Eight win was one of the greatest in Hoosier women's basketball history.

CHAPTER FOUR

All-Time Greats

Tyra Buss is the leading scorer in the history of the Indiana women's basketball program. She scored 2,364 career points, which is 400 more than the next highest scorer in school history. Buss is also the Hoosiers' all-time leader in steals, with 293, and **assists**, with 574. She played for Indiana from 2014 to 2018 and helped lead the team to the NCAA Tournament in 2016. She went on to join the coaching staff for the University of Wisconsin-Milwaukee Panthers.

The leading men's rebounder in school history is Alan Henderson. Henderson grabbed 1,091 rebounds between 1991 and 1995. He's also the eighth leading scorer in school history, with 1,979 points. Indiana made it to the NCAA Tournament each season Henderson played, going to the Final Four once and the Elite Eight once.

Tyra Buss, the women's Hoosiers all-time leading scorer, helped lead the team to the 2016 NCAA Tournament. ▶

THE G.O.A.T.

Guard Steve Alford played four years for the Hoosiers from 1983 to 1987. He led the team in scoring all four of those years. With Alford as the team's leader, Indiana went to the NCAA Tournament three times and won the 1987 National Championship. That year, Alford set a school record with 107 three-pointers. In the championship game, Alford scored 23 points, connecting on 7 three-pointers. Alford ranks second all-time in scoring at Indiana with 2,438 points, and second in steals with 178.

Forward Denise Jackson played for the Hoosiers from 1981 to 1984. She's Indiana's all-time leader in career rebounds, finishing with a total of 1,273. Jackson is also the school's second-leading scorer of all time, finishing her career with 1,917. Jackson set the school record with 22 rebounds in a 1981 game against Purdue. She earned a spot on the Big Ten all-conference team in 1983 and 1984.

Bobby Knight coached the Hoosiers' men's team for 29 seasons from 1971 to 2000. He was known for his energetic coaching style and for always having something interesting to say. But mostly he was known for winning. Knight ranks sixth in wins among all men's college coaches. He led the Hoosiers to three national championships. Only three coaches in history have won more titles. Knight's 662 wins are the most of any Indiana coach.

During his four-year NBA career, Steve Alford played for the Dallas Mavericks and the Golden State Warriors.

Point guard Isiah Thomas **started** every game he played during his two seasons at Indiana from 1979 to 1981. He led the Hoosiers to the Big Ten championship both years. In his second season, he led the team in scoring and set a school record with 197 assists. Thomas was the leading scorer in the 1981 National Championship game, leading Indiana to victory. He was named Most Outstanding Player of the 1981 NCAA Tournament. After college, Thomas went on to a Hall of Fame NBA career. As a pro, Thomas was a 12-time All-Star and led the Detroit Pistons to two NBA titles.

◀ **Indiana legends Bobby Knight (left) and Isiah Thomas (right) talk on the sideline. Together, they led the Hoosiers to the 1981 National Championship.**

CHAPTER FIVE

The Modern Era

The 2022–23 regular season was the most successful in the history of Indiana women's basketball. The Hoosiers finished with a 16–2 record in the Big Ten, winning the conference title. Overall, the team finished the year with a 28–4 record, setting a team record for most wins in a season. Although the team had high hopes for the NCAA Tournament, the Hoosiers lost 70–68 to the University of Miami in the second round. Coach Teri Moren won the Big Ten's Coach of the Year award after the team's amazing season. And senior forward Mackenzie Holmes was voted the conference's Defensive Player of the Year after tying for the conference lead in blocked shots. Holmes also finished second in scoring with an average 22.3 points per game.

In Coach Mike Woodson's second season with the team, the men's Hoosiers finished second in the Big Ten. Like the women's team, the Indiana men's squad also lost in the second round of the NCAA Tournament. They finished the 2022–23 season with a 23–12 record.

Indiana's Mackenzie Holmes launches a jump shot.

The men's team lost one of the top players in the history of the program in 2023. Senior forward Trayce Jackson-Davis was picked as an All-American after the season. He left Indiana as the school's third leading scorer, and the all-time leader in career rebounds and blocked shots.

With both the men's and women's teams losing top players to the NBA and WNBA in recent seasons, head coaches Moren and Woodson will have to depend on new leaders in the locker room and on the court. They'll have one of the loudest and most passionate fan bases in all of college basketball cheering them on!

TEARING UP THE LEAGUE!

OG Anunoby played two seasons for the Hoosiers from 2015 to 2017. A top defender, he helped the team win the Big Ten title and make it to the NCAA Tournament in 2015–16. Anunoby is one of the NBA's best defenders. In 2022–23, he led the NBA with 1.9 steals per game. He helped lead the Toronto Raptors to the 2019 NBA Championship for the first time in the team's history.

◄ **Trayce Jackson-Davis set numerous records at Indiana from 2020 to 2023.**

GLOSSARY

All-Star (ALL STAR) a player chosen as one of the best in a league, such as the NBA or WNBA

assists (uh-SISTZ) passes that lead directly to a basket

campus (KAM-pus) the grounds of a school or university

conference (KON-fuhr-enss) a group of teams that compete and play against each other every season

Elite Eight (uh-LEET AYT) games between the top eight teams in the NCAA Tournament

Final Four (FY-null FOR) games between the top four teams in the NCAA Tournament

NCAA (National Collegiate Athletic Association) a group that oversees college sports in the United States

NCAA Tournament (TUR-nuh-ment) a competition between 68 teams at the end of the college basketball season that decides the national champion

ranked (RANKT) placed on a list of individuals or teams that have accomplished high statistics in sports

started (STAR-tud) named as one of the players who is on the field or court when a game begins

Sweet 16 (SWEET six-TEEN) games between the top 16 teams in the NCAA Tournament

FUN FACTS

- Calbert Cheaney is Indiana's all-time points leader. He played for the Hoosiers from 1989 to 1993.

- Quacy Barnes graduated as the all-time leader in blocks for the Indiana women's team. In 1998, she became the first Hoosier ever picked in the WNBA Draft.

- Branch McCracken coached the Indiana men's team for 24 seasons between 1939 and 1965. He ranks second in school history with 364 coaching wins.

- Teri Moren passed Jim Izard's 188 victories in 2022–23 to become the leader in coaching wins for the Indiana women's team.

- The largest margin of victory in a women's basketball game for Indiana was in 1975. The Hoosiers beat Taylor College by 76 points!

ONE STRIDE FURTHER

- Some star college players, such as Indiana's Steve Alford and Calbert Cheaney, struggle to find as much success in the NBA as they did in college. Think about what might make someone more successful in college basketball, or more successful in the NBA. Write a paragraph about your opinion.

- Write a list of your favorite college basketball players. Include two things about each player that make them your favorite. Is it the way they play? Their attitude on the court? What else?

- Ask your friends and family members about their favorite sport. Keep track, and make a graph to see which sport wins out.

FIND OUT MORE

IN THE LIBRARY

Berglund, Bruce. *Basketball GOATs: The Greatest Athletes of All Time.* New York, NY: Sports Illustrated Kids, 2022.

Buckley, Jr., James. *It's a Numbers Game! Basketball.* Washington, DC: National Geographic Kids, 2020.

Hiner, Jason. *Indiana University Basketball Encyclopedia.* New York, NY: Sports Publishing, 2018.

Williamson, Ryan. *College Basketball Hot Streaks.* Parker, CO: The Child's World, 2020.

ON THE WEB

Visit our website for links about Indiana University basketball:
childsworld.com/links

Note to Parents, Caregivers, Teachers, and Librarians: We routinely verify our web links to make sure they are safe and active sites. So encourage your readers to check them out!

INDEX

Alford, Steve, 14, 22, 31
Anunoby, OG, 29

Big Ten Conference, 6, 8, 10, 22, 25–26, 29
Bloomington, Indiana, 4
Buss, Tyra, 20

Henderson, Alan, 20
Holmes, Mackenzie, 26–27

Jackson-Davis, Trayce, 29
Jackson, Denise, 22

Knight, Bobby, 6, 14, 22, 25

McCracken, Branch, 6, 31
Moren, Teri, 17, 26, 29, 31

Patberg, Ali, 13, 17–19
Purdue University, 10–13, 22

Smart, Keith, 14, 17

Thomas, Isiah, 17, 25

Woodson, Mike, 26, 29